Taking Care

A response to children, adults and abuse for churches and other faith communities

Helen Armstrong

The National Children's Bureau was established as a registered charity in 1963. Our purpose is to identify and promote the interests of all children and young people and to improve their status in a diverse society.

We work closely with professionals and policy makers to improve the lives of all children but especially young children, those affected by family instability, children with special needs or disabilities and those suffering the effects of poverty and deprivation.

We collect and disseminate information about children and promote good practice in children's services through research, policy and practice development, publications, seminars, training and an extensive library and information service.

The Bureau works in partnership with Children in Scotland and Children in Wales.

The views expressed are those of the authors and not necessarily those of the National Children's Bureau.

Original cover illustration by Matthew Rudd
Other illustrations by Clare Davies Jones

ISBN 1 874579 85 7

Published by National Children's Bureau Enterprises, 8 Wakley Street, London EC1V 7QE. Telephone 0171 843 6000

National Children's Bureau Enterprises is the trading company for the National Children's Bureau (Registered Charity number 258825)

Typeset by Goodfellow & Egan Ltd, Cambridge

Printed and bound in the European Union by Redwood Books

Contents

Acknowledgements iv

The author v

Preface to first edition vi

Introduction 1

Child abuse – what is it? 2

How to use *Taking Care* 3

Part 1: Background papers 9

1 A role for churches and faith communities 10
2 Child abuse: facts, figures and definitions 13
3 Responding to abuse: who does what? 15
4 Child abuse: issues for communities and individuals 17
5 Ten challenges to faith and practice 23

Part 2: Learning activities for groups 26

1 Is this abuse? 27
2 The child's view 29
3 Discussion 31
4 Case study 34
5 Check list for action 36
6 Difficult cases 37
7 The listening community 40

Part 3: What your community can do 42

1 Keeping children safe 43
2 Responding to a child in trouble 45
3 Ongoing care for children and adults 47

Appendices 50

1 Safe from harm 51
2 When a child tells about sexual abuse 53
3 Practical help and support for families 54
4 Resources for your community 55
5 Going further 58

Acknowledgements

The initiative for this material came from discussions between the staff of the Child Abuse Training Unit at the National Children's Bureau and members of the Consultative Group on Ministry Among Children. The idea germinated from an awareness of the particular role that churches of all denominations play in the life of the community and of the need for churches to develop their potential in responding to children in need. The first edition was published in 1991.

Taking Care was developed with an advisory group including representatives of Barnardo's, The Children's Society, The Methodist Division of Education and Youth, The Mothers' Union, NCH Action for Children, The National Christian Education Council, The Religious Society of Friends (Quakers) and The Salvation Army. Valued comment was also received from The Church of England Board for Social Responsibility and The International Ministerial Council of Great Britain.

The material was written and revised by Helen Armstrong. Additional material was supplied by Rev John Bradford, The Children's Society, Cathy Cooper, NCH Action for Children, Rev David Gamble, Methodist Division of Education and Youth and Anne Hollows, formerly of the Child Abuse Training Unit and now at the University of East London.

Those individuals who contributed to the development of this material by their advice and support include: Major Miriam Hart, Salvation Army; Anne Hosking, Religious Society of Friends (Quakers); Jenny Kimber, The Mothers' Union; Rev Simon Oxley, National Christian Education Council; Dr Elizabeth Penlington, Coventry Diocesan Education Committee; Mena Wilson, Barnardo's, Northern Ireland.

We would also like to acknowledge the comments and advice we have received from: Rev Don Black, Mission Office of the Baptist Union of Great Britain; Virginia Burton, National Council of Voluntary Child Care Organisations (NCVCCO); Mgr. M F Connelly, Catholic Child Welfare Council; Terry Connor, The Catholic Children's Society; Rev Phil Hoare, West London Methodist Mission; J A Hyland, Catholic Care North East; Rosemary Keenan, Catholic Social Workers Guild; Margaret Kennedy, East London Catholic Pastoral Area Office; Una Kroll; Rev Nicholas Monk, Parish of Minety, Oaksey and the Leigh; Major David Phillips, Salvation Army; Jim Richards, The Catholic Children's Society; Alison Webster, Church of England Board for Social Responsibility; Marguerite Valentine, Royal Borough of South Kensington Social Services; Annabel Warburg, The Children's Society and Liz Cowley, Early Childhood Unit, National Children's Bureau.

The author

The author, Helen Armstrong, is an independent trainer and consultant working with a wide range of organisations from small community based voluntary groups to national and statutory organisations. Her current work is an equal mix of direct training and production of training and learning materials.

From 1987 to 1992, she worked in the Child Abuse Training Unit at the National Children's Bureau, developing training and consultancy work with voluntary and statutory organisations. Since 1992, Helen has worked as an independent consultant. She has written and produced training materials in conjunction with the Open University, the National Children's Bureau and the Community Education Development Centre (CEDC). Helen has also worked regularly on Department of Health contracts with particular reference to the work of Area Child Protection Committees. Work in progress includes child protection training material for nurses.

Publications include:

Good Enough Training
With Anne Hollows. National Children's Bureau (1989)

Taking Care: A church response to children, adults and abuse
National Children's Bureau (1992) (The first edition of this book.)

Investigative Interviewing with Children
Open University (as consultant and contributor) (1993)

Child Protection For Health Visitors
HMSO (1994)

The Challenge of Partnership in Child Protection: Practice guide
Contributed the Team and Individual Training Exercises
HMSO (1995)

Your Guide to the Children Act
Department of Health
NCVCCO (1995)

A Safer Practice: Child Protection for Primary Health Care Teams
The Stationery Office and Department of Health (1996)

Preface to first edition

The care of children is a primary responsibility for us all, whether we are members of a religious community or not. It has become very clear over recent years that many children experience the pain of abuse and that it is often inflicted by those adults to whom they should be able to look for protection and love.

Child abuse is a major social issue for all of us. It is no longer possible to believe that the abuse of children only happens in certain types of home, or by easily identifiable individuals. We know that it can occur in homes and communities which are committed to life based on religious values and principles, as it does elsewhere in society.

Children everywhere need to know that the adults around them are able to respond sympathetically and effectively to help them. At the same time we know that many adults have experienced some form of abuse in their childhood and may still feel its impact. Those adults too need to feel confident of informed and loving support.

This publication provides church communities with a starting point for working with these challenging issues. It has been developed by a group representing several church traditions and it draws upon the professional expertise of the National Children's Bureau. I welcome this initiative, which will support much of the valuable work already being done in churches.

John Reardon
General Secretary
Council of Churches for Britain and Ireland

Introduction

Taking Care provides church communities with a sensitive and straightforward way of considering the issue of child abuse. Since its first publication in 1991 it has been used as the basis of work and study in churches at local, regional and national level.

This new edition has been thoroughly revised to take account of new research and recent developments in work with children at risk and their families. It includes updated information on abuse and on the professional response, together with new and revised activities.

Taking Care was initially developed by representatives from different traditions within the Christian church. Its content and design, however, mean that faith communities of other world religions are likely to find it relevant to them in caring for the children in their midst. For simplicity in some parts of the text we refer to 'churches'. We are very aware that this term may not be in line with the structure and name of the faith community of many who use this material nor does it represent the range of world religions found in the UK and elsewhere. We hope you will bear with this 'short-hand' which is made necessary by the lack of an all-embracing term for the variety of groupings which mark religious life.

Taking Care provides:

- information about child abuse;
- information about the professional response to children at risk of abuse and in need of help;
- learning activities for groups;
- guidance on practical steps faith communities may want to take to protect children and support families in stress;
- information and advice on responding to adults with childhood experience of abuse or adults involved in abusive situations.

A good way of reducing the likelihood of child abuse or of unhappy children is to ensure that parents feel secured and valued. Within this framework of loving support a lot can be done to help us all improve the ways in which we nurture and educate our children. *Taking Care* has been written to help faith communities broaden their sympathetic understanding of children and families. It is not written to fuel anxieties or encourage criticism of the way parents raise and care for their children.

We are aware that there are dangers in presenting this material to groups which do not have the support of professional networks nor a background of professional training. Nonetheless, experience with the first edition of *Taking Care* has demonstrated that communities can address the issue of child abuse very effectively when given the opportunity to reflect about it together, particularly with informed guidance from leaders who are thoroughly prepared.

We wish to record as a framework for this publication, the obvious truth that relationships between children and adults, whether within faith communities or outside these communities, can be a great source of strength and joy for all concerned. Nothing said here should be allowed to cloud our knowledge of the value of that relationship.

Readers of *Taking Care* will be vulnerable to strong personal responses to the many destructive aspects of child abuse. The impact of child abuse is destructive in many ways and may be felt 'at second hand' by others. It can stir up all kinds of feelings in unexpected ways. It is important for you as an individual to identify people and groups with whom you can share your feelings. If you are working with a group, careful thought needs to be given to ensuring that all members of the group can receive this kind of support.

Child abuse – what is it?

- Zeta is ten years old. She knows she is stupid because her parents tell her so. She doesn't do well at school. In fact she doesn't do well at anything. Her mother once told her that she wished Zeta had died as a baby and often behaves as though Zeta wasn't there. When the family goes out, Zeta is left behind because she 'always lets them down'. Zeta has given up trying to be clean or tidy; it is no good. Even the children at school seem to think she is not the same as other children and won't play with her. Last week she stole some chocolate from the shop because eating helps when she feels so unhappy.
- Mark is 11. He is often beaten by his Dad. It is because he is such a naughty boy, his Dad says. One day Mark shouted at his Dad to stop and got such a clip over one eye that he hasn't been able to see properly with it since. He had to tell the doctor he had been hit by a football. He often thinks of running away.
- Fiona is very careful. She is four years old. She always watches her Mum and Dad. She never knows what they are going to do. She hates it when they begin shouting because it may be her turn next. When the hitting starts, she tries to keep out of the way but it often doesn't work. Last week she was thrown against the wall and hurt her head. She was sick afterwards.
- Laura is six years old. When her parents go out in the evening, her cousin Robert babysits. He is 14. Over recent months he has come into her room when she has gone to bed and climbs into bed with her. He says he has new games to play – 'our secret game' – and she must not tell anyone. He says that if she tells he will let his dog kill her guinea-pig. She has always thought her cousin was wonderful but she doesn't like this new game and she hates it when he says frightening things. She is very confused and is becoming tearful and nervous.

Child abuse, whatever the circumstances, damages and restricts a child's physical, mental or emotional development. We have started with the experience of children – the rest of *Taking Care* suggests ways in which we can hear what these children need to say; how we can notice that something is wrong even when children can't say; and ways in which we can get help and security for them.

How to use *Taking Care*

The different parts of *Taking Care* provide different resources – for work in groups, for individual reading and for discussion. How you select the activities and reading will depend upon your local circumstances.

Part 1: Background papers

These papers are designed to give information and to highlight important issues. They can be photocopied for reading before group sessions or given out for follow-up or used as the basis for group discussion. These papers are particularly useful to group leaders in preparing summaries for presentation to the group, but will also help the individual reader.

Part 2: Learning activities for groups

Learning activities are designed to help groups raise their awareness of how they and their local faith communities can meet the needs of children in trouble and their families. This section is designed to be worked through from Sheet 1 to Sheet 7, but it is quite possible to select a smaller number of activities.

Part 3: What your community can do

This section is also designed for use in groups. It offers questions and suggestions for those who are responsible for organisation within the faith community and pastoral work. It is important that everyone tackling these questions has first participated in at least some of the activities in Part 2.

Appendices provide:

- details of additional materials;
- information on agencies offering help;
- suggestions for further work;
- a sheet suggesting ways of listening to what a child may have to say about sexual abuse.

Leading groups

It is important that groups working through this material have the help of informed and careful leadership. Group leaders using this material will need to have:

- a knowledge and experience of children and families, their problems and difficulties;
- knowledge of the issues of child abuse;
- knowledge of the professional system for protecting children;
- some experience of leading groups;
- awareness of the ways in which adults learn;
- some level of listening and counselling skills.

There are important advantages in having two leaders for any group working on this material. It allows for a much wider spread of skills and knowledge. It also means that one person can lead an activity while the other takes the role of helping and supporting individuals. Such an arrangement also allows mutual support for the leaders.

An example of a useful spread of leadership qualities could be to have one leader with professional knowledge in the subject area and a second leader with involvement or strengths in the life of the local faith community. There are many other useful pairings.

It may be possible to find these skills within your local membership but in many cases it will be best to look for advice and support from the wider church organisation, or from the local sources of help such as the social services department of your local council or the NSPCC. In some localities, groups of churches or faith communities may find it useful to organise shared sessions.

Learning in groups

Taking Care can be used for individual learning, but it is chiefly designed to be used in groups. Here, we suggest some ways in which the different parts of this material can be brought together into short programmes for local groups.

Practical matters

You will need to look at the practical aspects of leading a group including:

- good access for all, including those with mobility problems;
- timing that suits your group;
- suitable facilities, and a choice of refreshment;
- space for working and security from interruption for your group;
- flip chart or large working sheets of paper for activities plus marker pens;
- enough copies of necessary case studies and information sheets.

Care for group members

When you have made outline plans for the group, you need to give thought to the welfare of all taking part.

It is advisable to agree, at the beginning of the first session, on the need for confidentiality about what is said within the group.

It is possible that several people in any group will be distressed by aspects of the material. There may well be one or more members of any group who have personal experience of abuse. This experience is likely to have been (and still be) a very troubling and important event in their lives.

Distress may not be about an experience of abuse – it may be anxiety about family life, about their failure to protect a child in the past, about their ideals of human behaviour or deep anger. It may be about feelings or about re-thinking long cherished beliefs. Different situations will need different responses.

At the end of this section is a page headed 'Information notes' and we strongly advise that you write in the contact for local or community sources of support and give copies of this sheet to all members of the group as you start the first session.

After sessions, and sometimes during sessions, be prepared to allow time if an individual needs to take a break or needs someone to talk to. In a few cases more long term support may be required and you need to plan for how best to meet this kind of need should it arise.

Leading sessions

It is important to make everyone welcome at the start of each session – child abuse is a disturbing topic and group members may feel some natural anxiety. It is wise to make time for proper introductions at the start of the programme. Assumptions that everyone knows each other may be inaccurate. Each session also should be brought to a clear 'close'. For many groups a final prayer or few minutes' quiet thought will be considered appropriate and helpful.

Overall group size is also important. In general it is sensible to limit groups to a total of no more than 12 people. Where the group is meeting in a home, a total of eight to ten people will be a large group and will need careful organisation.

The activities in Part 2 of *Taking Care* work best when the work is done in small working groups of perhaps three to five people. These small groups can 'feed back' their views to the whole group. In this way individuals get a chance to voice their feelings and ideas even when the group is a large one.

Who needs to learn about child abuse?

The community as a whole

Everyone in a faith community needs to be aware of the existence of child abuse, of how it may come to their attention, and how to respond. It is important that the community as a whole feels a responsibility for the welfare of the children in its midst and for troubled adults. This is likely to mean that discussion groups on the topic of child abuse are advertised widely within the community and are open to all. Local faith groups need to assess whether this is appropriate in their own community.

Leaders

Some individuals, often leaders in the faith community, such as ministers or priests, may be approached by members of their community who have anxieties about children they know or about their own situation. This places a great burden on such individuals who are unlikely to have specialist knowledge in the area of child protection. It is vital that such leaders feel able to contact the local social services child protection team or their local branch of the NSPCC, and that they are clear that this is their duty to children at risk. Establishing friendly links with these organisations is a useful step.

Named individuals

Some faith communities may feel that they want to identify 'key individuals' for people to go to with anxieties about children or families. These individuals will need additional preparation and considerable support. Both leaders and 'named individuals' will need help in clarifying their role. Their task is not to investigate but to place the needs of a child above any painful repercussions for adults; to seek official help or advice; and to mobilise the resources of the community to support children and families in need.

Choosing your programme

Your selection of information and activities will depend upon your assessment of the needs and experience of those in your group.

For some groups you will be aiming at general awareness-raising sessions. For others you may be helping a small task group to make decisions on their procedures. Each situation will mean selecting a different mix of information and activities.

There are other practical points to consider, for example, where one, or more, members of the group has a communication difficulty or a disability. It is also important to give attention to the level of reading skills within your group, which can vary widely.

Here we give listings of the material in *Taking Care* to suit different groups and different needs. You will probably wish to select from within these listings but you may decide that a completely different mix of information and activities will suit your group best.

An introductory course: Programme 1

The material listed here can be used over one, two or even three sessions, depending on the time available. These elements will be suitable for a general awareness-raising introduction to the topic of abuse. They also form an important basis for those who wish to complete a fuller programme.

Contents

1 Each participant should be given a copy of the Information notes (p. 8).
2 Complete Activity 1 – *Is this abuse?*
3 Give a short presentation using Paper 2 as your basis.
4 Complete Activity 2 – *The child's view.*
5 Complete Activity 3 – *Discussion.*
6 Complete Activity 4 – *Case study.*
7 Go through Activity 5 *Check list.* Note outstanding questions for future consideration.
8 Give out Paper 3 – *Responding to Abuse: Who Does What* for discussion or reading at home.
9 All participants should be given a copy of Appendix 3 – *Practical help and support* for their information. Appendix 2 may also be relevant.

For groups interested in looking broadly at the work of their faith community, we recommend planning a follow-up session or sessions using Activity 7- *The listening community.* This activity is relevant both to the whole community and to those with responsibility for planning local policy (see Programme 3 below).

Further work: Programme 2

The material listed here is designed to look at the more troubling and difficult issues raised for faith communities by child abuse. It can be used in a single session after the completion of all or part of the materials in the Introductory Programme.

Contents

1 Read and discuss Paper 4 – *Issues for communities and individuals.*
2 Complete Activity 6 – *Difficult cases.* Note outstanding questions for future consideration.
3 You may wish to include material from other resources, perhaps one of the videos listed in Appendix 5.
4 Appendix 2 may be relevant.

Organising your faith communities: Programme 3

These materials are designed for consideration by those with responsibility for setting policy and procedures for your faith community. Before undertaking this programme, all participants should have completed all or part of the work in Programmes 1 and 2. Any outstanding questions from this previous work should be available for consideration at this meeting.

Contents

1 Preparatory reading of Paper 1.
2 Read or present Paper 3 – *Responding to abuse – who does what?*
3 Work through Part 3 of *Taking Care – What your community can do.* This sets a framework for three sessions:
   1 Keeping children safe (for this session you will want to use Appendix 1 as a framework for planning action.)
   2 Responding to a child in trouble.
   3 Providing ongoing care for children and adults.

Spiritual issues: Programme 4

This programme is for those within Christian churches who wish to give fuller consideration to the spiritual implications of responding to child abuse. These groups will wish to give detailed attention to the topics raised in Paper 5 – *Ten Challenges to faith and practice.* We recommend that this consideration should follow completion of Programmes 1 and 2 as listed above. In addressing Paper 5, groups may wish to plan a session for each of the topics raised, or give individuals responsibility for introducing each topic.

Information notes for group members

This group is meeting to share thinking about the issue of child abuse and our response as a faith community.

Child abuse is a painful subject. In the course of the discussion, you may find that personal memories are brought to mind; you may feel very powerful emotions of anger or disgust; you may think back and remember with anxiety a child you have known whom you feel you have failed. Such feelings are the natural result of considering this topic.

Should you wish to talk over these thoughts and feelings in confidence after the session, please contact:

....

You may wish to ring ChildLine 0800 1111, which offers a listening ear to all troubled by abuse, whether child or adult.

You may also, if you prefer, ring local helplines such as the Samaritans, who are available in many areas on a 24-hour basis.

Strong response to child abuse is both natural and fruitful. Without it there would be no action to help children or adults who have felt the impact of this damaging experience.

Part 1

Background papers

1 A role for churches and faith communities
2 Child abuse: facts, figures and definitions
3 Responding to abuse: who does what?
4 Child abuse: issues for communities and individuals
5 Ten challenges to faith and practice

Background paper 1

A role for churches and faith communities

The role of any faith community with regard to children at risk lies in supporting troubled families to prevent abuse; listening to children when they wish to talk; referring immediately to social services or NSPCC where abuse is suspected; providing long-term loving care to all involved in damaging and abusive experiences.

It is essential that any thinking and learning done in local faith groups about abuse is not seen as a way of avoiding involving the proper authorities in cases of suspected abuse. Abused children can only be protected through calling in those with the power and resources to help them and their families.

Hearing 'bad' news

Much of *Taking Care* is about being prepared to listen to 'bad' news. Children need to be able to talk about the painful bits of their lives as well as the happy bits. Adults too need to be able to talk about things that trouble them even when hearing about them disturbs the listener. Caring for children and adults where family stress and abuse are issues, means bearing the pain and difficulty and working through it, rather than avoiding it. This is a major challenge for all of us in faith communities.

Why the churches?

Churches and communities of all faiths are unique in what they offer because of their place in society. Members of such communities share a commitment to the spiritual welfare of members and non-members alike. They share the important tasks and joys of their lives – especially the birth and nurture of their children. Members look to their church or faith community for guidance and example in good parenthood.

It is clear that child abuse is a very destructive experience for all concerned. Where child abuse has happened, there is often a need for healing and nurture if individuals are to grow past and through the experience in a positive way. No community is exempt from child abuse and churches therefore have a responsibility to prepare themselves for a well-grounded response.

It is very painful to have to believe that abuse of children may occur within our faith communities themselves. As members of such groups, we may feel that we are all committed to caring for the welfare of others and being sensitive to their needs. Abuse is the opposite of this – a deliberate over-riding of the needs of one individual to meet the needs of another. Yet abuse does happen everywhere. Whatever our ideals for ourselves, many of us are damaged by early experiences, limited by aspects of our lives, or driven by inner stresses. Within all faith groups there is a need to approach the possibility of the existence of abuse within our own group or within our own lives, in a spirit of alert humility.

For many people who are not members of church, or who perhaps look to the church or faith community only at points of transition or crisis, it represents a particular kind of help and strength. It is at points of change and crisis that people are likely to need to talk about abusive experiences. All members of such communities need to be prepared to meet such individuals with belief, understanding and a capacity to listen and respond.

A community of faith may also find itself treated as a source of informed comment within its locality on personal and social issues such as child abuse. It is quite common for local radio stations or newspapers to seek the views of leaders or members when difficult and painful issues arise. Those in membership of such communities will need to have reached informed, compassionate and considered views on child abuse if they are to offer helpful comment at such times. This is an additional responsibility for leaders to consider.

We may not be able to envisage bringing about the end of all abuse of children. But faith communities can ensure that they are powerful influences for the kind of education which reduces its likelihood. They will want to provide safe and nourishing environments for all children, and for the adults those children become.

Exploring feelings

One of the most important steps for adults working in this field is to explore and recognise their own feelings about abuse and to begin to deal with those feelings. Everybody who works in this field needs to know it is perfectly normal to feel distressed and bewildered. Indeed it is important to retain the capacity for such distress if we are to remain sensitive to the nature of the experience.

It may seem self-indulgent to think about how *you* feel about abuse of children when it is obvious that it is the *children's* feelings which matter most. But if you consider the child who wants to tell somebody about their abuse, you will realise that they need to talk to someone who is not visibly shocked, who does not make them feel that they must be guilty of something terrible, and above all someone who will listen and believe them. In fact the child needs someone who has thought about their own reactions in advance and has prepared themselves to listen and to act in an appropriate way. It is never possible to be completely prepared but adults have a responsibility to have at least partially worked out their own responses if they are to meet the needs of children in trouble.

There is an added difficulty for adults in a child's confusion of feelings about the abuse and the abuser. A child may still love the abusing adult despite fear or distress about the abuse. The child may, in cases of sexual abuse, have felt some physical response which makes them feel they share the responsibility.

This can be a major part of the distress caused by abuse, and is likely to prove equally difficult for adults who hear an account of abuse from a child. Adults need to respect all parts of the child's experience of abuse while believing in the innocence of the child's role.

Many adults have experienced abuse in some form, and discussions about the issue may revive old memories in a painful way. This is part of the challenge of abuse and faith communities need to be sure that they can support and care for individuals through all their discussion activities. One of the most worrying aspects of thinking about abuse is that you may even find in yourself feelings about children or young people which you now feel might be similar to those leading to abuse, perhaps a capacity for extreme anger, or some sexual feelings. Recognising such feelings is painful but part of coming to a realisation that we all share the capacity to feel emotions and stirrings to action which we would condemn, and that abuse occurs where such feelings are allowed to extend into action.

Changing the way we think

A church or community of faith can be an ideal forum for everyone to work out a rationale of childhood, of sex, of maturation, of adult and parenthood responsibility, of crime and punishment, forgiveness and reconciliation. Careful preparatory work which brings thinking about child abuse within the overall spiritual thought of such a community can help this process considerably.

Thinking about child abuse has a strong impact on how you see the world and how you think about people. You may begin to 'see' abuse everywhere, or you may lose confidence in the basic goodness of human nature. Child abuse is a disturbing subject and may lead you to re-think much of what you have accepted without question in the past.

Knowing more about abuse may also lead you to review some actions you took in the past – perhaps a child whose needs you ignored, or a situation you participated in where you now wish you had acted differently. Although thinking about past events may not seem useful, it can lay the foundation for changing how we act in the future.

Rethinking our view of the world and of ourselves is a difficult but important stage to go through. Knowing more about child abuse does change how you think about people. All those committed to a religious view which values each individual and their potential for good, will need to share their thinking and feelings about abuse. They will need to work towards a new understanding of the world which includes acceptance that many human beings hurt and use children. Yet they will want to bring to that understanding a commitment to love and healing for all concerned.

This is not easy and while working through these shifts in their perceptions, group members may find themselves troubled by ideas and feelings with which they need help.

Preventing abuse

Much abuse can be prevented by timely support for families.

Churches and other faith communities may be able to provide practical resources to support families going through stressful times. Where financial pressures or a poor home environment are adding to other stresses, the offer of a warm comfortable place to go, a hot meal, the chance for children to share playing time, and the support of caring adults can be a vital lifeline through troubled times.

Where mental health problems, or abuse of alcohol, or drugs, play a part in putting children at risk, such communities are likely to have a supportive role to play, in conjunction with professional help to the family.

Such help at the right time, whether from the whole community or from a caring individual, can prevent abuse before it happens, and provide opportunities for the whole family to come through bad times without lasting scars.

The rewards

Using this material in local faith communities is bound to raise some difficult feelings, but there are substantial rewards. Looking at these topics allows us to reflect on the whole way in which members support each other and care for each other through the difficulties every individual experiences. Facing up to and working through the issues raised, can lead to a closer, more caring and fuller life for the community. And this in itself is a good mirror of how we can help children and adults move through bad experiences to healing and growth.

Background paper 2

Child abuse: facts, figures and definitions

Defining kinds of abuse

These definitions of different 'kinds' or categories of abuse are taken from Government guidance *Working Together Under the Children Act 1989* (marked WT) and the Open University course *Child Abuse and Neglect 1989* (marked OU).

'Physical Abuse: where a parent (or somebody else caring for the child) physically hurts, injures, or kills a child. This can involve hitting, shaking, squeezing, burning or biting. It also involves giving a child poisonous substances, inappropriate drugs and alcohol and attempted suffocation or drowning. It includes the use of excessive force when carrying out tasks like feeding or nappy changing.'(OU). 'Actual or likely physical injury to a child, or failure to prevent physical injury (or suffering) to a child.'(WT)

'Sexual abuse: when adults seek sexual gratification by using children (girls and boys). This may be by having sexual intercourse or anal intercourse (buggery), engaging with the child in fondling, masturbation or oral sex; and includes encouraging children to watch sexually explicit behaviour or pornographic material, including videos.'(OU) 'Sexual exploitation of a child or adolescent'. (WT) Another definition by Schechter and Roberge, American authorities in the field of sexual abuse, states that sexual abuse is the 'involvement of dependent, developmentally immature children or adolescents in sexual activity they do not fully comprehend and to which they are unable to give informed consent, or which violates the social taboos of family roles'.

'Neglect: where parents (or whoever else is caring for the child) fail to meet the basic essential needs of children, like adequate food, clothes, warmth and medical care. Leaving young children alone and unsupervised is another example of neglect. Refusing or failing to give adequate love and affection is a case of emotional neglect.'(OU) 'The persistent or severe neglect of a child, or the failure to protect the child from exposure to any kind of danger, or extreme failure to carry out important aspects of care, resulting in the significant impairment of the child's health or development.'(WT)

'Emotional abuse: where children are harmed by lack of love and affection, by threats and systematic bullying, by constant verbal attacks and taunting. Emotional abuse may lead to developmental delay as well as psychological damage.'(OU) 'Actual or likely severe adverse effect on the emotional and behavioural development of a child caused by persistent or severe emotional ill-treatment or rejection.'(WT)

What is child abuse?

Child abuse is a general term used to describe the ways in which a child's development and physical and mental health are damaged by the actions of another person, usually an adult. The Children Act states that where a child may suffer 'significant harm', action must be taken to protect him or her. The Act states that harm may arise from ill-treatment and/or impairment of health and development. Government guidance describes abuse under the four categories listed above.

For a child, the experience of abuse often includes harm of several kinds. Any form of abuse brings with it an element of emotional abuse. Physical abuse and sexual abuse may occur together. Neglect, which may be easier to overlook than some other forms of abuse, can be very damaging to a child's development in the long term.

Many abusive acts are carried out by adults very close to the child – parents, relatives, close family friends, and other members of the child's immediate circle.

How common is abuse?

It has never been easy to know how much child abuse there is and we do not know whether abuse is more common than it used to be or simply more often identified. Many adults report abuse in their childhoods which received no attention at the time. Current figures suggest that between 50 and 100 children die each year as a result of abuse or neglect. Research provides evidence that perhaps one child in ten may suffer from some kind of sexual abuse during his or her childhood.

How do you recognise abuse?

A concern about possible abuse may be triggered in several ways. You may hear a comment from a child or adult; you may more rarely be told details of abuse by a child or adult; you may notice an injury which suggests abuse; or you may observe behaviour that causes you concern. It is rarely the case that you can be 'sure' that abuse is happening or has happened. Almost always one piece of information is not sufficient and this is why professional agencies work together and share information when responding to concerns about a child.

Abuse in your community

Experience and knowledge of child abuse is likely to exist within your church and/or community whether from personal experience or more indirectly. Some people in your church may be dealing with cases of abuse in a professional capacity as social workers, teachers or doctors. Others either as individuals or perhaps as members of a local voluntary group, may be supporting families. There will almost certainly be members of any church or faith community who have experienced abuse themselves.

Responding to children at risk, means drawing upon the experience, the skills and the commitment of your community and deciding what you can do together to help keep children safe.

Background paper 3

Responding to abuse – who does what?

The Children Act

The Children Act 1989 became law in England and Wales on 14 October 1991. The Children Act covers the whole field of child care law and includes provisions for protecting children. The Act says that children must be protected where they are at risk of 'significant harm' and this means ill-treatment and/or impairment of health and development. The Children Act stresses that where there are grounds for believing a child is not safe, enquiries must be made. The Children Act is part of civil law and is implemented through the civil judiciary. In Scotland the relevant legislation is in the Children (Scotland) Act 1995 and in Northern Ireland covered by the Children (Northern Ireland) Order 1995.

The Criminal Law

The Criminal Law is a separate body of law designed to prosecute offenders. It is comparatively rare for a case involving child abuse to come to trial in a criminal court. Such cases often rely on children giving evidence and experience shows that there are many difficulties in children giving effective evidence in a criminal trial. A child may therefore be given protection under the Children Act without there ever being a criminal trial of the person who is suspected of abusing the child.

The Area Child Protection Committee – ACPC

All the chief agencies working with children and families in your area are members of the Area Child Protection Committee. The task of this committee is to make sure that professionals work together effectively to protect children locally. The 'lead' agency in this process is the local authority social services department. This means that when you as an individual or as a church have concerns about the safety and welfare of a child, you need to contact your local social services child protection team. (In some areas social service departments have other titles – your local council can help you in identifying who to go to.) In some areas there will also be an NSPCC team who will be able to help.

Keeping children safe

The Children Act says that all reports of concerns should be taken seriously **but** this does not mean that a telephone call will result in a full multi-agency investigation! Social services departments have a legal duty to make enquiries where a child may be at risk. In many cases these early enquiries will lead to no further action or to the offer of family support services. In a comparatively small number of cases (approximately one in four) a child protection conference will be called so that professionals from all the relevant agencies, together with parents and sometimes children, can share information, assess the risk to the child or children, and plan a response if they decide that a child is at risk.

Government guidance stresses that parents should be partners in this process wherever possible and should be closely involved in making sure that their children are safe. Children too, should be encouraged to make their views heard.

The importance of family life

The Children Act sets a high value on the child staying with his or her own family so it is only if all other measures have failed that a child will be removed from his or her home and placed in a foster home or other accommodation. Of all the children referred each year, less than one in a hundred are urgently removed from the family for emergency protection. Sometimes after the conference stage, a decision may be made to remove children. Families may agree to temporary alternative care for their child on a voluntary basis. All these children (under four per cent of all referrals) will return home wherever that is possible and as soon as possible.

Preventing abuse

Since the passing of the Children Act there has been a growing emphasis on preventing abuse before it happens. The Act set out responsibilities for local authorities to identify and support 'children in need'. Increasingly families where children are at risk of abuse are seen as in need of support services. This is an important shift which may make it easier for churches and other faith communities to feel that in acting to protect children they are taking positive steps to nurture and support a family in distress.

Of course support is not the whole answer. Sexual abuse may occur in families where there is no obvious need for general support. Severe physical abuse may mean that professionals need to take immediate and urgent steps to protect a child. Nonetheless in many cases timely help and support can mean that children can stay with their families and be safe.

Questions for churches

Churches may have families in membership where it is felt that a child is at risk of some form of neglect and abuse. Adults within the community may be living under a suspicion of abusing a child, whether physically, emotionally or sexually. On rarer occasions a church or community may have in membership an individual with a criminal conviction for abuse or who has admitted abuse, and who wishes to be a full and active member of the community. Each situation is different. Each is painful and may raise disturbing questions for church members.

For each church or community a responsibility must remain towards all the individuals concerned. This will often present great difficulties and will require considered and prayerful response. At the same time such communities must be careful not to attempt to take over the proper roles and responsibilities of the professional agencies.

Background paper 4

Child abuse: issues for communities and individuals

Any case of child abuse will raise particular issues for those who come into contact with it. These may be about abuse itself; about how abuse affects individuals; or about how the church or faith community responds. It is important to have given time to considering these issues in preparation for dealing with a case of child abuse because they can give rise to strong feeling and practical difficulties. We have summarised some key issues here but there may be others.

Confidentiality

It is essential that members of faith communities refer suspicions and evidence of abuse to their local social services department or NSPCC. It is also important that appropriate members of the community are alerted so that they can respond to possible abuse in an effective way. However it is equally important that a proper degree of confidentiality is observed. The personal situations of individuals should not be made public without their consent. The tension between necessary sharing of information and respect for individual privacy needs to be thought through carefully before a crisis, and a policy agreed and publicised.

Child-centred ways of working

Structures of faith communities can often be adult orientated. The ways in which children are respected and valued in such a community will affect a child's ability to feel confident to talk in that environment about his or her own experiences. Children need to feel that their views and choices are respected and that they can refuse to participate in unwelcome invitations from adults.

Personal responses

Work in this sphere often has a considerable personal impact on all involved. Faith communities should develop support systems for people who are encountering child abuse. Supporting those involved is likely to make great calls on time, unshockability and one's inner resources. What is needed is a supportive environment where difficulties can be shared frankly and the right kind of pastoral care given. This may mean opportunities for confidential one-to-one support from an informed person or a support group. Such support must of course recognise the involvement of the authorities in work with the child and family.

Gender and power

On present evidence it is considered that men are responsible for about 90 per cent of all sexual abuse, and the majority of physical abuse. Abuse of whatever kind is an abuse of power. Adults and children who have been abused may find it difficult to feel comfortable with male authority figures. This has particular relevance to faith communities, where positions of power are largely held by men (though child care is often the preserve of female members of the community). It is important to ensure that those in need can locate women with the necessary authority to respond effectively. More widely it raises questions as to how the 'maleness' of the authority and power structure can be modified. Women do abuse children too, most commonly either physically or emotionally.

Physical punishment

There is a fine line between physical punishment and physical abuse of children. There is evidence that one way to prevent abuse would be to outlaw physical punishment of children. In countries where this has taken place there has been a marked decrease in physical abuse of children, over a period of a few years. This raises questions for each church on how it helps parents to develop ways of maintaining discipline within the home which do not run the risk of becoming abusive.

Adult survivors

The scale of child abuse now known to exist must mean that children in earlier generations, who may now be parents or even grandparents, were themselves abused and have never had the opportunity to talk about or come to terms with what has happened to them. Sometimes their feelings about the abuse and their memories of what happened have been buried deep in the past and it is only in hearing contemporary accounts that they begin to recall what happened to them in their childhood. Faith communities need to be aware of this for two reasons. Firstly they will want to be able to provide pastoral care for such adults in their community and secondly, these adults may find themselves confronting abuse in a child and may be unable to respond appropriately because of their own experience.

Children and adults with disabilities

Children with disabilities are very vulnerable to being abused, physically, sexually and emotionally. They may have greater difficulty communicating information about the abuse and they may be less able to resist. They may, in addition, feel more excluded from the faith community than children in general. It is difficult but important to look for ways to communicate with children who may not have a full range of communication skills open to them and to encourage children with special needs into full membership of the community.

Young adults with learning difficulties or other disabilities continue to be vulnerable to abuse of all kinds. Research statistics show a high rate for sexual abuse in particular. This seems to relate to the higher numbers of adults outside the family who are involved in providing care for such young people. Adults who abuse people with learning difficulties, depend upon their victim's inability to report the offence or to be believed if they do.

Sometimes a disability, in child or adult, can be the result of abuse. Severe physical abuse may cause a variety of physical disabilities and may lead to brain damage. Sexual and emotional abuse can also mean that a child's development is affected, particularly in their ability to learn and communicate.

Young people or adults with learning disabilities may occasionally sexually abuse others younger or weaker than themselves. This behaviour requires careful professional help. At the same time of course the child or adult who has been the victim of the assault, who may themselves have a disability, needs appropriate support and assistance.

Abuse of boys

Evidence suggests that boys are sexually abused almost as frequently as girls. It has been suggested that boys who are sexually abused have particular difficulties in admitting that they have been 'victimised' because of the expectations our society has of boys and men. Research also suggests that boys are more often abused outside the family than girls, and may more often be victimised in organised networks of abusing adults.

Boys are more likely than girls to be physically abused, particularly under the age of 11.

Organised networks of paedophiles

In many parts of the UK there are networks of people who are sexually attracted to children. Individuals in such networks will target situations and groups which allow them access to children. Faith communities may attract such people because they offer the possibility of moral authority over children and easy access. Paedophiles are adept at disguising their true intent and church organisations need to be alert to this possibility.

Some networks of abusing adults may use ritual objects and ceremonies to frighten children and make them keep silent. This experience may be particularly terrifying for children at the time and later as they grow into adulthood.

Sexual abusers

Sexual abuse happens in all parts of society and in every cultural and ethnic group.

Experience and research demonstrate that more men sexually abuse children than women. On the other hand women do sexually abuse children, sometimes on their own and sometimes with men.

Some of those who sexually abuse are only attracted to children; some to both children and adults. Some victimise only boys or only girls; many however will abuse children of either sex. There are some abusers who fit the popular stereotype of a man with limited social skills and difficulty in establishing adult relationships. Many others have apparently satisfactory adult relationships and may be married with families. Fathers and stepfathers who sexually abuse their own children may also abuse children outside the family. Where women sexually abuse, they too may victimise their own children or others. Some abusers are confident, articulate individuals who may be respected in their communities and be particularly noted for their ability to 'get on with' children and young people. Research has shown that some abusers over a life-time will sexually abuse several hundred children.

As much as a third of sexual abuse is carried out by young people under 18 years of age, and even by quite young children. For some of these young people, abuse will be a temporary deviation. For many, unfortunately, it is the beginning of a pattern and unless offered early help they are likely to go on to a lifelong 'career' of abusing.

Many adults with a history of abusing children have never been prosecuted and convicted. This means they have no criminal record.

Evidence suggests that those with a history of sexual abuse have considerable difficulty in changing their pattern of behaviour. Many show little motivation to do so. Some however do succeed in changing direction and churches will wish to support such endeavours though with a degree of caution. One way of understanding the urge to sexually abuse children is to think of it as an 'addiction'. It may be helpful to remember that many faith communities would certainly warmly support someone overcoming alcohol addiction but they would not give them unrestricted access to alcohol. A similar prudence and care for others is needed in responding to 'reformed' abusers. Respect for the safety of children must guide all decisions in this regard.

Children who abuse

The high proportion of sexual abuse carried out by young people means that faith communities need to be alert to the risks of using youngsters in unsupported care of younger children, a situation which is likely to be undesirable in other ways.

There is evidence that young people who show sexually abusive behaviour to other children may often have been abused themselves. In such cases the abuser is therefore also a victim and will need professional treatment for both sets of experiences/behaviour. Although there is a concern about describing children as 'abusers' it is important to recognise that children and young people may cause serious damage to younger or weaker children. It is essential that early help and treatment is offered to young people who sexually abuse others as it is clear that early abusing can be the start of a lifelong pattern.

Physical and emotional abuse, which may be passed off as harmless bullying, is also widespread and damaging. There is now much more awareness about the long term psychological (and physical) harm bullying can do. Churches and faith communities will wish to make sure that any behaviour of this kind is checked at the earliest stages, opposed as it is to everything that makes such a group a community of caring people.

Ethnicity

Abuse of all kinds can happen in any social and cultural setting. It is always a negative and destructive experience. It may however be even more difficult for those in minority communities to call in outside help from the statutory agencies, which may perhaps be perceived as part of a hostile or racist system. It is also true that where there is experience of prejudice or stigmatisation because of ethnicity, the experience of being abused may compound those feelings. In some parts of the country, community leaders from ethnic minorities are involved in initiatives to ensure that children of all ethnic groups have equal access to help and protection from abuse.

Forgiveness

For Christian churches, forgiveness is of central importance. Sometimes a church community may ask that a victim of abuse forgives his or her abuser as a first step. This can cause serious difficulties particularly where the abuse may be secretly continuing or where the victim has not yet been able to express all his or her anger and grief at what has happened to him or her. Churches may wish to consider their response to this with particular care.

Religious language and the experience of abuse

Abuse, particularly sexual abuse, raises questions about the nature of the 'family', about what a 'father' is and what the parental role is. Religious language often depends on a positive view of the value and trust placed in fathers, parents and the family. For an abused child (or an adult with childhood experience of abuse) there may be real difficulties in this type of theological language which may have an effect on the child's spiritual life. For the abused child confusion may arise between the language in which the spiritual life is presented and the experience such language aims to represent.

Children who have been incestuously abused often feel great anger and bitterness (mixed with other emotions) towards the father or other relative, who abused them. Many children who have been sexually abused within the family, are also very angry that they were not protected by those close to them and this anger is often directed at their mother. These feelings may not be fully recognised but may lead to strong reactions against traditional language which represents God as Father or as protector, or indeed to the range of 'family' language used in religious thinking.

The child may be frightened to acknowledge these feelings but may need help in understanding the role of such language. These issues need handling with care and sensitivity.

Issues for individuals

Believing children

Children who have reached the point of talking about abuse need to be believed. This can present real problems for adults who foresee all too clearly the consequences of believing the child, such as hostility from their community, disbelief, losing the trust of adult friends. It helps if adults have thought about these anxieties beforehand and preferably talked them through with others. They also need to be quite clear about the practical action required from them in these circumstances. This preparation frees them to take effective action. The fact that children are usually abused by adults who are close to them makes belief no easier for other adults whose own families may be 'safe' places, but it makes believing and protecting the child yet more vital.

Childhood experience

Most adults can remember times when as children they felt powerless against adult wishes. Dealing with abuse can mean that the adult begins to share the child's sense of powerlessness. It is crucial that adults retain awareness of their own power to change things and to act to protect this child even if they feel that they themselves were often unprotected when they were children.

Sexuality

Sexual abuse raises issues of sexuality for all who become involved. It often brings to the surface the memory of unhappy sexual experience, sexual anxieties, confusions and ignorance about sexual activity. It is quite common for an adult who is working with a case of sexual abuse, to experience difficulties in his or her personal sexual life. This is usually short-term and adults involved may need reassurance on this.

Sexualised behaviour in children

Some children who have been sexualised at an early age by sexual abuse, may involve other children in sexual activities and games. They may also make sexualised approaches to adults. Adults need to demonstrate their loving care of abused children by clearly maintaining the boundaries between affection and sexual contact of any kind. It is vital that children who have been taught to behave in a sexual way prematurely, be helped to re-learn the normal boundaries of behaviour between people. This learning will help re-build their sense of worth and self-respect.

Same-sex abuse

Boys who have been sexually abused by men may suffer anxieties and confusion about their sexual identity which they find difficult to share. Almost all sexual abusers are men and many of these, in fact, abuse girls or boys without discrimination. However for the boys who experience the abuse it may raise fears that the abuse indicates that they are, or will inevitably become, homosexual as an adult and this may cause them concern. More generally boys often feel great confusion about being 'used' in what they see as a female role and need help in re-establishing male identity. These anxieties will be additional to all the other repercussions for the individual which are part of sexual abuse. Those working with abused boys need to feel at ease with open discussions of these anxieties.

Abuse by an adult of the same sex is not uncommon and has been reported, though much more rarely, between women and girls. It always causes confusion and adults should be prepared for their own reactions in hearing of such cases, while remembering that the child's needs must come before their own difficulties.

Background paper 5

Ten challenges to faith and practice

by John Bradford, Missioner, The Children's Society

In relating

1. Respecting the child or young person

The first challenge concerns the principle of respect for the intrinsic worth and value of each child. Any form of abuse is a denial of this unique worth and dignity of each young life, and of the respect which that demands. It is important that children and young people are included as full participants in the worship, discussion and practical life of a church since this symbolises their equal membership and significance as an individual. In such a context the possibility of any form of child abuse should be absolutely minimised.

2. A haven for restoration

The second challenge is to remember that while a church may not be able to 'cure' a particular situation, it has a primary role in providing a safe, healthy and caring environment which offers a victim (or abuser) space for healing and re-orientation. It should also be remembered that it may be very difficult for a child or young person to relate to adults who are of the same sex as the abuser, and due 'space' for choice and distance in encounter should be allowed.

3. Affirming care professionals

The third challenge is for a church to affirm and support social workers or other care professionals who may be members of the congregation and to allow the church life and worship to be a natural source of inspiration and refreshment for them in their day-to-day managerial or case work. A church forum may provide a helpful means of opening up certain ideological dilemmas arising from such work.

In teaching and learning

4. Promoting a broad personal and social awareness

The fourth challenge is for churches to be learning communities – encouraging the development of wholeness through building up positive attitudes and understanding towards a wide range of issues, including sex and sexuality, reward and punishment, parenthood and parental responsibility, childhood and the rights of the child, confrontation and rehabilitation. Only a church community which is both a prayerful and an instructed community can begin to handle the multiple and deeply upsetting issues raised by a single incident of child abuse.

5. Addressing issues of culpability and guilt

The fifth challenge is for a church community to be clear about the general underlying principles of its moral base – how to discern between behaviour which is right and that which is wrong; and also to be clear about their church's teaching and ministry of forgiveness and of the thinking behind this. Occurrences of child abuse tend to have a pressing immediacy and to evoke a sense of outrage which make it particularly desirable that steady religious thinking about moral values and their application has already been taking place.

In the Christian tradition, some questions illustrating principles of rightness will include: 'Is what I am doing pleasing to Christ?', 'Is what I am doing promoting Christian love (agape)?', 'Is what I am doing contributing to the building up of the Body of Christ?', 'Is what I am doing giving dignity and self worth to a fellow-member of God's kingdom/of God's family of mankind?'. Child abuse in any form meets none of these criteria.

Special consideration must be given to the fact that an abused child or young person will invariably have suffered the transference of guilt from the perpetrator. A child or young person should never be allowed to suffer under, still less be ministered to in respect of, a guilt which is in no way theirs.

6. Educating for wholeness in family life

The sixth challenge for a church is to engage in teaching and learning about parenthood (children being a gift and not a possession), and the process of family life in association with the church (including helping young people to full independence and responsibility). Parenthood should be accepted as both a relationship of trustful affection and a form of service – not a relationship of exploitation and the abuse of power.

7. Giving constructive support

The seventh challenge is that any church may have among its membership, or involved in one of its associated activities, someone who is or has been a perpetrator of abuse. A church has to act with great prudence, confidentiality and responsibility in affording not only an appropriate context for worship but also a just and appropriate pastoral response. The task of a church will be neither to needlessly and intrusively interfere with a situation with the risk that it may deteriorate still further, nor to take flight from its pastoral responsibilities but to accept them and work at them. Two fundamental issues are:

- Within our limitations, how do we listen to and support a child or young person who is or has been the victim of any kind of abuse, and help them to come to terms with what they suffer and feel?
- Within our limitation, how do we help someone to acknowledge their wrong doing and help that person to change. Are we suitably aware of other appropriate avenues of help to which we could discuss referral?

8. Sharing in ministry

The eighth challenge is to have a shared ministerial style. A church which seeks to befriend and protect a child or young person who is experiencing abuse in some form is wise if it encourages the collaborative ministry of members of both sexes, with appropriate skills and insights, and possibly liaises with other church or church related agencies which might offer specialist guidance or support.

9. Offering devotional therapy

The ninth challenge is for a church to act as a channel to allow the victim of abuse to bring the pain, sorrow and contamination of abuse of any kind to a suitable prayerful, liturgical or symbolic expression in order so far as possible for the sufferer to be free from the indignities, sense of uncleanness and torturous memories from the past.

10. Providing opportunities for reflection

The tenth challenge to a church is to be open:

- to all children having some recognised way in which they can have access to a responsible and suitable adult or group with whom they can speak or consult when they are in difficulty;
- to adults having some constructive way of reviewing their family life in the tradition of their church; and of exploring and examining the strengths and weaknesses of the pattern of family life with which that church is most identified. In such a forum problems can come to the surface and dangers can be prevented.

Part 2

Learning activities for groups

1 Is this abuse?
2 The child's view
3 Discussion
4 Case study
5 Check list
6 Difficult cases
7 The listening community

Activity 1

Is this abuse?

Notes for group leaders

It is easy to think that 'child abuse' is clear cut. In fact people do not always agree about what is abuse and what is not.

Aim

This activity is designed so that people in your group can think about some of the complexities of identifying and responding to 'abuse', including defining what is abusive.

Organising the activity

Ask the group to work in pairs with the activity sheet. Ask them to write 'OK' against the statements they think are not 'abuse'. They should put an 'A' against those they do consider abusive. Please note, that with regard to the question about shaking a baby, whatever the result of the group's thinking on whether it is abusive, it is certainly very dangerous and likely to cause permanent damage (and therefore significant harm) to the baby.

Now check out with the whole group – have they all come to the same decision? Do they disagree on any of these examples? For several of them the response may be 'it all depends' – in other words more information is needed. It is helpful to point out that this reflects ordinary life where a concern about abuse may arise in a situation which is far from clear. This is why the child protection system puts so much emphasis on sharing information and working together.

After the activity, ask group members to say on what grounds they decided which examples were abuse. By pooling these ideas, you may be able to come up with this group's definition of abuse. It is important to inform the group that the ground for protecting children under the Children Act is that the child is suffering or likely to suffer 'significant harm', rather than on the intention of the abuser or any other factor which they may find important to their own definition.

Please note: in some cases members of the group may disagree strongly about one or more of these examples or may have strong reactions to a particular example. Be prepared for this possibility, ensuring for example that there are two group leaders and that you have considered your responses carefully.

Activity sheet 1

With a partner, go through these statements and write 'OK' against those which you think are not obviously 'abuse'. Put an 'A' against those you think are 'abuse' or may be abuse. Is there anything you disagree on with your partner?

Now check out with the whole group – have you all come to the same decisions? Do you disagree on any of them? For several of them you may say 'it all depends'. In other words you need more information – this is what the child protection system does. It shares information so that people can be more sure.

Is it abuse when . . .

- a four-year-old is locked in his room for an hour for wetting his pants?
- a 12-year-old is slapped hard with a hand?
- a baby is shaken by its mother?
- a father sleeps in the same bed as his 12-year-old daughter?
- a mother sleeps in the same bed as a 14-year-old son with a disability?
- parents walk around the house naked in front of the children?
- a mother tells her young son that she wishes he had never been born?
- a 12-year-old boy forces a seven-year-old girl to masturbate him?
- a man persuades a 10-year-old into sexual acts by offering affection and money?
- a 13-year-old boy is beaten with a belt for telling lies?
- a six-year-old girl is left on her own at home, for several hours every night while her mother goes out to work? Or when her mother goes out with her friends?
- parents decide not to allow their under-five child to have toys because they like a tidy house?

How did you decide? What makes one thing abuse and another not? Note down some ideas here.

Activity 2

The child's view

Notes for group leaders

This activity draws on the four case studies on page 2 and is designed to give a clear focus on the child's experience and needs. It is very easy for adults to take more notice of the plight of other adults and you should try to help groups keep their thoughts on the child for this activity.

Aim

This activity gives people the opportunity to think out what abuse may mean for a child, short or long term.

Organising the activity

Divide your group into four working groups and give each the task of looking at one of the case studies. Each group will need a copy of the question sheet overleaf. After about ten minutes, draw them together for feedback and discussion.

Activity sheet 2

Think carefully about the situation of the child in your case study. Those of you working on the case which involves two children (Laura and Robert), should focus mainly on Laura and give attention to Robert if time permits.

A Write down what you consider this child will feel – at this moment – as a result of this experience:

- about him or herself?

- about adults?

- about other children?

- about family life and parenting?

B Think about the future. How do you feel that this child may be affected as he or she grows up?

You may want to consider how things may be different if for example the situation was identified and professionals intervened; or alternatively if things go on much as they are at present.

C In the event of someone getting to know about this situation, consider how your faith community might be able to contribute to this child's safety and welfare, now and in the longer term?

Activity 3

Discussion

Notes for group leaders

This information sheet is designed to be read and discussed in a group.

Aim

This discussion ensures that all group members have clear information on their role in responding to abuse.

Organising the discussion

You may find it convenient to hand out copies to read before the session or to work through it paragraph by paragraph with the group. This can be helpful to those who may not find it easy to read and absorb a document rapidly.

Activity sheet 3

Information for discussion

The experience of a child

Children depend upon adults for care and for their safety. They need to be able to trust adults to have their welfare at heart. Abuse of any kind shows a child that they cannot trust adults in this way. Often a child who is abused may be forced to 'keep this a secret' by threats or by violence. They may feel isolated and think that no-one will believe them if they do try to speak out.

An experience of abuse will affect the way a child understands the world and the people about them, which means that it necessarily affects their lives as adults. Many abused children can go on to full and productive adults lives but skilled help may be needed to make this possible.

Your responsibilities

If a child is being abused it means that an adult (or older child) is using their power or strength to harm that child. Children can rarely protect themselves. Adults outside the situation need to take action.

You may suspect abuse from observing a child or an adult's behaviour, or noticing an injury. Sometimes you are told directly about abuse or about actions that sound to you abusive.

Sometimes either child or adult may begin by asking you to promise that you will tell no-one else. You cannot make that promise. When you have heard what they have to say, you may decide that you have to report what you have heard, to keep a child safe.

It is important to remember your own responsibilities and the limits of your responsibilities. It is not your job to 'find out' the details of what may have happened. Your job is to be alert to the possibility of abuse, to listen and to support until the appropriate agencies can take over. And then to go on supporting.

When to respond will vary depending on what you think is happening to the child. Children are killed or permanently damaged by physical attacks: these situations must be urgently and immediately reported. Where you suspect that a child is being hurt emotionally or by sexual approaches, you may feel you would like to discuss the grounds for your concerns before making a formal referral. Some social services departments are open to discussions about a concern before it becomes a formal referral. There is also a free national NSPCC Helpline, which is open 24 hours a day to give expert advice to those concerned about a child's safety. The telephone number is 0800 800 500.

Talking to your social services department usually means ringing your local council and asking for the child protection team. If there is an NSPCC team working in your area you can contact them. The telephone numbers will be in your local directory or your local Citizen's Advice Bureau will be able to give you the right number to call. In some urgent cases you may wish to contact the police.

What happens next

In many cases early enquiries by social workers and others make it clear that concerns were not founded and no further action will be taken. In other cases, professional support may be given to the family. In a few cases, a full enquiry will take place. Of course even when a child is considered safe from abuse, both child or family may need all the support which their church community is able to give them.

Activity 4

Case study

Notes for group leaders

This case study provides the opportunity to think about the situation of a child in trouble in your own locality. Before starting on this exercise it will be helpful if members of the group have discussed the range of experience which come within child abuse. Copies of the definitions from Background paper 2, will be useful.

Aim

This case study is designed to allow the group to draw upon their own experience of families and the community and to think carefully about how a child in difficulty may seek help and which adults may become involved in giving that help.

Organising the activity

Divide into groups of four to five. Each group will need a large sheet of paper and a thick pen to draw a 'map' like that shown below. You may find it useful to demonstrate the diagram on a flipchart first.

Allow 10 to 15 minutes. Now you can ask the group to consider how their answers and suggestions might be different if Holly wanted to say that her father was sexually abusing her. This is not likely to change her contacts but will often change how people feel about responding and reporting the case.

Allow five minutes. Now ask all groups to feed back and share. Discuss.

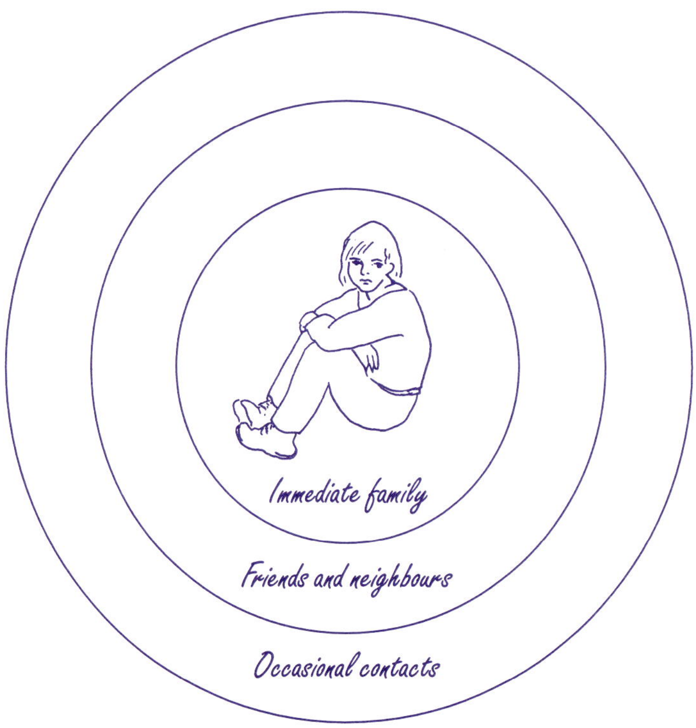

Activity sheet 4

Case study: For group members

Holly is 10 and goes to the local school. She is the eldest of four girls and lives with her father and mother. From time to time the whole family attends church.

Holly always looks very different from her sisters. She is often rather dirty, pale and worn looking. She does not seem as bright and lively as her sisters and it is clear that her parents feel she is a disappointment to them.

1. **Who is likely to be close enough to Holly for her to talk to them about her personal circumstances? (Draw these people on a 'map' like the one on page 34 .)**
2. **Other questions you could consider:**
   - Is there anyone within the church she might be able to talk to?
   - Would these adults know what to do if it became clear that Holly was being neglected and possibly emotionally abused?
   - What action could they take?
   - Who is in a position to supply long term support and help to Holly and her family over the next months and years. What kind of help could be offered?
   - Where might the helping adults find their own support?

Do your answers to these questions suggest any areas of action for your church community

Activity 5

Check list for action

What do you need to know?

This sheet can be used as a check list for individuals or groups. Much of the information can be drawn from Activity sheet 2. However the situations of each individual and the local setting will mean that there can be useful discussion of what the answers would mean in your community.

- **Where**, within the life of your church, may you encounter a child in need of help?

- **Who** would you tell? There may be someone you would confide in. Who would you have to tell for protective action to be taken?

- **How** would you inform the authorities? Do you know who to contact?

- **What** would you expect to happen next? Would you expect to be kept informed or to be further involved? How would you see your longer term contribution? How could you handle the situation if you do not get any feedback or further contact?

Activity 6

Difficult cases

Aim

To allow for shared consideration of some of the difficult issues arising from cases of abuse.

Organising the activity

Divide participants into working groups of two or three people. Give each group a case study plus a question sheet to consider. Use a range of case studies over the whole group. When all the groups have had time to work on their case (possibly 20–30 minutes) they can share their thinking with the whole group. Finally, everyone can share ideas on what these cases might suggest for action within their local church or faith community.

Activity sheet 6

Case studies

A Rob (14) has always attended church with his family. He was sexually abused at the age of eight by an uncle who then introduced Rob to a group of men and boys where he was further abused. Two years ago, the men seemed to lose interest in him and since then he has been lonely and increasingly confused. He is worried about his sexual fantasies – they don't seem the kind of things people at school talk about – and he believes that he is homosexual. He is sure his family and the church would think he is wicked. Today in church he feels desperate. He decides to try to talk to the minister after the service.

B Carole is concerned that her husband Brian frequently beats her elder daughter (seven) for trifling errors, singling her out from the rest of the family. She has dropped hints to her friends in the young wives group that Brian is hard on the girl, but no-one has taken her comments seriously. She doesn't know what to do.

C Ben (eight) is very interested in music and often goes to watch Mark the organist while he is playing. Ben admires Mark who is a local personality and the musical mainstay of several local churches. Today Mark lets Ben touch the keys and promises to teach him some more next time. Then he draws Ben aside and touches him under his trousers in a way that frightens the boy. Mark tells Ben that this bit is a secret and his parents wouldn't understand or believe him. Then he goes with a flushed and upset Ben to tell Ben's parents that he will begin to teach the boy the organ.

D Jeff was beaten by his own father who believed that to spare the rod spoilt the child. Jeff now does the same to his own son, Michael, who is six. Jeff is sometimes so angry that he gets 'carried away' and on more than one occasion Michael has had to have time off school as a result of a particularly heavy beating. To the chapel community who know the family well, Michael seems a rather wild, erratic child who has a lot of trouble concentrating on anything for more than a very short while. One day he shows a bruised arm to one of the other children and the adult helper is called over.

E Clive (12) has attended church since a baby with his family. For the last few years he has been a bit of a bully with younger weaker children when he is in a group. Last week he frightened a little girl by touching her sexually behind the church building after the service.

F Ryan (four) was a late and unexpected addition to the family. He is not as bright as his three much older brothers. His mother, Donna, is hostile to him. She can hardly bear to be alone with him although she tries to conceal this. Ryan knows his mother doesn't like him. He is developing slowly for his age and the health visitor is concerned about his lack of progress. There are days when Donna gets upset and locks Ryan in his room, sometimes for hours. She knows this is wrong and tries to think of someone she could ask about feeling like this.

G Lucy (nine) who attends church with her parents is very troubled because her best friend at school has described to her something horrible that her father is doing to her at home. Lucy promised not to tell her parents but is very distressed and frightened by what she has heard. She wonders if the lady running the Sunday morning children's group might be able to tell her what to do.

Activity sheet 6

1. **Imagine you are the person who is chosen to be told about this problem or who finds out about it.**

- What do you feel about the situation of the child or children in this case?
- What do you feel about the adult(s) (if there is an adult in your case study)?
- What is the worst that could happen to the child or children if nobody takes action?
- What feelings or difficulties might make you hesitate in taking action?
- What feelings would make you take action, no matter what problems followed?
- Are you clear about what you should do? Does your church or faith community have a clear policy which helps you take action? As an individual, do you know how to contact your local social services department?

2. **Over the months and years following these events, consider how you and members of your community could help the individuals concerned, both children and adults.**

- What might this involve?
- What would be your aims?

Activity 7

The listening community

Notes for group leaders

These two activities are designed to help participants in the group draw upon their experience of their faith community to reflect on how far support and help are available to both adults and children.

Responding to the needs of children at risk and their families, means first and foremost being prepared to listen and to hear what they have to say. This is not always easy. Children and adults under stress are often not able to communicate their need for help or support. Faith communities may be busy with little time for quiet listening to each other. These activities are designed to help your community think about ways to make it easier for listening to take place.

Activity 7A is best completed first by individuals followed by sharing of general ideas and conclusions.
Activity 7B is best carried out by small working groups.

Aim

To allow group members to reflect on the support provided by their faith community and how this can be improved

Organising the activity

For both activities introduce by emphasising the value of being a ‘listening community’ as outlined above.
Activity 7A: Hand out the activity sheet. Ask each participant to spend a few minutes reflecting on the first part of the activity – thinking what kind of response they might expect for ‘bad’ news. Share ideas around the group.
Then ask the whole group to consider the listed questions. Finally focus on the last question ‘What can be done?’ Work towards producing three practical suggestions that may make support stronger and more accessible.
Activity 7B: Each small working group needs a large sheet of paper and a thick pen to draw their ‘line’. Demonstrate how the line can be drawn with marks for each person the child meets.
Ask each group to consider a child of a particular age. Allow 10 minutes for completion and then share the results. Finally ask the whole group for ideas on how the community could make it easier for a child to have time to talk about things that worried them.

Activity 7A

Hearing 'bad' news

The following exercise is best done by individuals.

In many communities the birth of a baby, a wedding or a new job meet with warm congratulations. There may even be a community celebration. More difficult news – a marriage breaking up, a poor health prognosis, the loss of a job, acute money problems – may not be so easy to respond to. Think about how you might find support within the community when your news was 'bad news'.

For the group

- How can you all become more prepared to hear 'bad' news from people in the community?
- How can members of your community identify who can help them and who might be willing to help and support them in times of trouble?
- What can be done in your community to make the response everything you would wish?

Activity 7B

Being a child

You are a child walking into your local place of worship. Draw a line for your 'path' up to and into the building and during your time in there. Mark on the line every person you could expect to meet, marking those who would certainly greet you. Now think about who you might get time and opportunity to talk to if there was something troubling you. *If you are working in several groups you may wish to choose to be a child of different ages – for example one group 'be' a four-year-old, one an eight-year-old and one a twelve-year-old.*

Discuss with others and see how the situation might be improved.

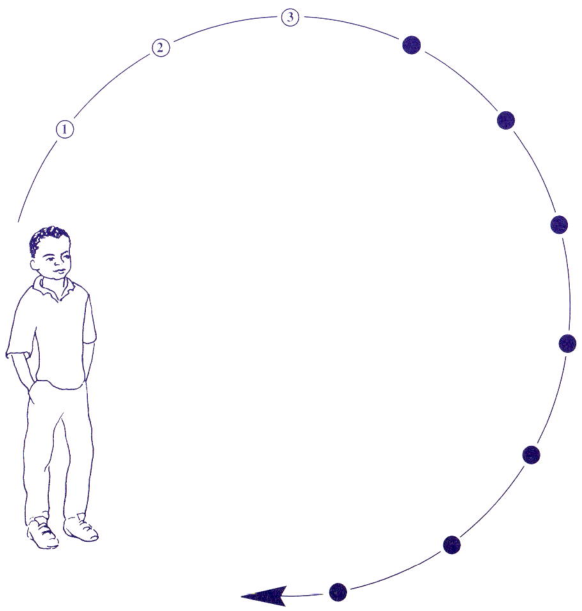

Part 3

What your community can do

1 Keeping children safe
2 Responding to a child in trouble
3 Providing ongoing care for children and adults

1 Keeping children safe

All churches and faith communities will wish to keep children safe. This will mean making sure that children are safe from harm within the boundaries of your community itself. More widely it will include helping to make children more safe in other aspects of their lives including their homes. This means listening to children, making them feel valued, and offering support where families are going through difficult times.

Safety in church

The government publication *Safe From Harm* gives guidance on how to keep children safe. Taking the advice of that publication, you may wish to ensure that policies are in place which cover the practical issues of checking those wishing to work with children, supervision and the organisation of activities. Developing these policies and putting them into action may mean changing the way things have previously been done.

Questions for discussion

These questions are designed for general discussion. A practical checklist is given in Appendix 1.

1. Organising work with children

- How you can make sure that children are always in the care of two adults when away from their parents.

- If this is not possible, how can you ensure that other adults are within easy reach and preferably in sight?

- What can you do to encourage children to know that they can approach other adults (perhaps a named adult) and that they will be sympathetically listened to?

Children may be at risk wherever they are in the sole charge of an adult, particularly where they are separated from other adults. However, setting up a policy to avoid this may cause difficulties within the community. Some people may feel that they are being suspected of wishing to harm children or that the fabric of trust within the community is damaged by this approach. These concerns can often be allayed if the policy is clearly based upon *Safe From Harm* which itself reflects the fact that these measures have become necessary with increasing knowledge and experience of abuse.

These precautions also protect adults from suspicion or from misunderstanding about their behaviour towards children. Remember you need to consider every activity, not just those you may think of as 'children's activities'. Wherever children are involved, their safety has to be a priority. It may mean rethinking choir meetings, bell ringing or gardening. For special events too – perhaps evening events or residential trips – you need to be sure you have thoroughly considered the safety aspects for all concerned. At the same time, be ready to react promptly to changes of plan or last-minute alterations by those who are leading such events.

2. Recruitment of children's workers

- Have you given due consideration to how you recruit people to work with children?

It is rarely possible for local churches to get a police check on previous criminal offences. In any case this would only tell you about convictions and most people who abuse children do not have convictions. You can take practical steps though to make sure that those wishing to work with children are checked in other ways.

- Do you ask volunteers questions about their experience and background, and do you ask for references and take them up?

In recruiting volunteers or staff wishing to work with children, it is helpful to be able to show them a clear policy statement that you are a 'safe church' and that you therefore do take up references and operate the kind of rules described above. This statement is helpful to you and will also act as a signal to any who wish to take improper advantage of access to children, by warning them that you are an alert community aware of potential risks.

The wider task – preventing abuse

3. Giving children a voice

- In what ways are children in your community encouraged to express their views and allowed to talk about their lives and feeling? What kind of decisions or choices can they be helpfully involved in?

- Do you think that children are likely to feel that they are listened to and that there is always someone to talk to if they wish to share anything that worries them? Have you asked them?

- How can you work to make the situation more encouraging for children?

You may want to consider new activities and approaches in your work with children, which emphasise the value of the children's voices and views. It may be helpful to organise sessions with children as part of their normal learning programme in which they have the chance to share their lives, including difficulties, with adult members. These sessions could help children to identify adults they can talk to easily.

This kind of work with children could be used to lay foundations for fuller sharing among adult members and the growth of a more trusting community. Parents and those who lead children's educational and social activities should be invited to support and plan such a programme.

4. Supporting families

- How do you think your local church and faith community can help support a family when it is clear that there are problems and stress, even when there is no question of the children being abused in any way?

- Do you think your community is sensitive to the way long term stress can build up in a family? Is there anyone an anxious parent can speak to or go to for practical help?

2 Responding to a child in trouble

Churches and faith communities need to develop clear guidance which is familiar to all members of that community, on how any adult should act when encountering abuse or suspicion of abuse. It will often fall to the minister or priest to guide the next steps for the child's benefit. However it remains every individual member's personal responsibility to ensure that where abuse is suspected, suspicion is reported to the local social services child protection team or to the local NSPCC. Responding effectively needs preparation.

Questions for discussion

1. Church members

- How can members of the church or faith community become more aware of their responsibility to help children in trouble? Do you feel that it might be useful to draw up a straightforward advice sheet on how to respond to suspicion of a child in trouble or danger? If so how would you make sure that the guidance was followed in practice?
- Do you think it is useful to name one person as a source of advice?
- What would this mean for them? What kind of support and preparation would they need?

2. Preparing those who work with children

All those who work with children need to be prepared for the fact that a child could talk about abuse or fear of abuse during church or community-based activities. Children may also describe behaviour at home or outside the home that sounds abusive to the listener.

- How do you think you can prepare people for this?
- Are there any parts of *Taking Care* that you could use?

3. Meeting the needs of a child

- How will the children in your community know who they can go to?
- Are there ways in which you can help them work out who they find it easiest to talk to?

It will be useful to check which individuals you identified during the Learning Activities as having a good contact with children in your church or faith community. These may not be people with an official role.

4. Building links

- How could you begin to increase your knowledge of the local professional response to children in trouble?
- Do you think it would be useful to make contact with the local social services child protection team or NSPCC team to establish a link which will make contact easier in future should the need arise?

5. Helping families

- In what ways can your church or faith community be more of a help to families in trouble?

- Are there ways of providing long term support whether there is an immediate crisis or not? These could be practical help or listening and caring support – ideally both.

Where abuse is suspected, there may be situations where a parent with his or her child urgently needs temporary shelter which members of your community can offer. More problematically there may be times when it is right to offer accommodation for someone suspected of abuse. This does however have attendant risks. It may be seen by the child and others to reflect a pre-judgement of that person's innocence. Where the individual has abused, there will be ongoing risk to other children. Churches and communities may decide that it is better to support alternative accommodation for the adult.

6. Offering learning resources

- Would it be useful to consider building a small library of materials? This could contain books for adults and for children.

- Can you foresee difficulties and what kind of control do you think might be necessary in holding these materials and making them accessible? Communities could consider giving copies of useful books (such as the *Courage to Heal* workbook) to those they know are survivors of abuse. Such books are often not cheap and may be beyond the pocket of individuals.

3 Ongoing care for children and adults

The kind of long term healing and support needed in cases of child abuse will depend upon the nature of the abuse, whether the abuse is recent or in the past, and whether the child, family or even abuser are members of the community. Different situations will require careful consideration of the most effective forms of help available from the community. Some of the main aims of such work are outlined below.

To help child and family

Where child abuse has been identified in a family attending or in membership of the Church, the situation may be widely known in the church community. Where action has been taken by appropriate authorities, the situation may still not be satisfactory or clear cut. Whatever has happened there remains the long term task of care and support for all involved so that healing can take place and the children and adults involved have help in 'growing through' their experience.

In some cases there may be a suspicion of abuse which is not definite enough to lead to action. It may be that initial enquiries by social services and other agencies are inconclusive. This may leave a continuing doubt about the safety of a child or about the behaviour of an adult. Ongoing care for children and adults is vital in this type of situation. Whatever the original cause of concern, there may now be additional feelings, possibly of anger or resentment, which will be affecting the family. All members of the family will need support. Whatever may have happened in the past, supportive help to the family is the best insurance against future problems.

To help the child

Where a child is suffering from the effects of abuse, including emotional abuse or neglect, the church may be able to offer effective help by giving the opportunity for that child to feel loved and valued, to have fun, and be part of a group which is supportive and caring. This alone will contribute to the healing process.

Helping and caring for a child who has experienced abuse of any kind may not be easy. Children who have been abused can develop difficult patterns of behaviour as a result of their experiences, and this behaviour may persist for a long time.

Opportunities to include the child in activities need to be sought and followed up. For many children, there is also a need for specialist help and churches ought to consider their role in making this help more accessible. In such situations, churches will wish to liaise with the specialist helpers for guidance on the best forms for their own supporting activity.

To help adults

It is possible that within the church there may be adults who were abused as children; there may be a parent involved in an abusive family and under considerable stress; there may even be an adult who is currently abusing children, either their own or more widely.

- An adult with childhood experience of abuse of any kind may find that a major life event such as a parental death, marriage, or birth of a child, or an encounter with an abused child, may cause them to recall their own experience. They will need understanding and support available from other adult members of the community, to help them through what may be a very troubled time.

Appendices

1 Safe from harm

2 When a child tells about sexual abuse

3 Practical help and support

4 Resources for your community

5 Going further

Appendix 1

Safe from harm

The Home Office has published a guide for voluntary and community groups on how to protect children, called *Safe From Harm*. This important publication can be obtained by sending a cheque for £2.50 (payable to the Home Office Accounting Officer) to the Publications Unit, Home Office, 50 Queen Anne's Gate, London SW1H 9AT.

For groups who wish to follow the recommendations in *Safe From Harm*, we suggest the following check list. This list includes the recommended areas within the Home Office publication, organised into action topics. These action topics can be used as a checklist by those responsible for pastoral work in the local church or more widely as a basis for discussion.

Keeping children safe check list

Action topic 1: Preparing those who work with children

This means making sure that all who work with children are aware of abuse and clear about their procedure for responding to possible abuse.

- Have you prepared all who work with children to be aware of the possibility of abuse?
- Are all your volunteers (and staff) clear about the procedures for making a referral if this should be necessary?
- Have you got a system for recording concerns where they arise?

Action topic 2: Barriers to abuse

This refers to the ways in which your community can put barriers in the way of anyone who wishes to use your community to harm children.

- Do you have a policy statement which makes it clear that you are committed to taking all necessary steps to protect children?
- Do you always give a copy of this statement to those who apply to work with children?
- Do you always ask for and take up references?
- Do you make use of any checking system open to you locally or nationally?
- Do you have a 'probation period' to make sure that volunteers and staff are suitable for this work?

Action topic 3: Organising your work

This means organising your work with the safety of children in mind.

- Do you make sure that a sole adult is never left alone with a child or children? If this does happen do you ensure that someone outside the situation has an overview of the activities?
- Do you avoid situations where a child or children leave the premises in the care of one adult without access to others?
- Do you make sure that someone has responsibility for monitoring all work with children, and that this monitoring is carried out in an open and direct way with full knowledge of all involved?

Action topic 4: Giving children a voice

This means making sure that all children you care for and work with as a faith community, have access to someone other than their immediate carer and that they know who they can contact.

- When children are with your faith group, are they told who to contact outside that situation, if they need to for any reason?
- Are children in general helped to talk about themselves and their situations and feelings to sympathetic adults?
- Are adults in your community likely to be welcoming and open to children who wish to talk? Do you have any system for helping or supporting adults in this approach?

Appendix 2

When a child tells about sexual abuse

It is not possible to write down exactly what to do when a child tells you about sexual abuse. The points below are offered as guidelines, and to aid discussion.

General points

- Look at the child directly.
- Try to keep your eye level equal to or lower than the child's.
- Do not promise confidentiality.
- Assume that the child has been threatened.
- Help the child to trust his or her feelings.
- Try to find out what they are afraid of, so that you will know how best to help.
- Make notes as soon as possible. Try to write down exactly what the child said.

Helpful things to say

- I believe you.
- I am glad that you told me.
- I am sorry that it happened.
- It is not your fault.
- I care, and I will help.
- You were right to tell, and it is OK to tell.
- You were brave to tell.
- The abuser was wrong. (It is better not to say 'bad'.)
- Even if the child has broken a rule, he or she is not to blame for the abuse.

Try to avoid saying

- Why? How? When? Where? Who?
- Are you sure?
- Why didn't you say before?
- I can't believe it.
- Statements such as 'This is really serious'. 'Don't tell anyone'. 'I am shocked'.
- False promises.

To finish

- Tell the child again that you believe him or her.
- Let the child know what you are going to do, and, as far as is possible, what is going to happen next.
- Praise the child for telling, and for surviving the abuse.

Women's Support Project, Newhouse Centre, 871 Springfield Road, Glasgow G31 4HQ
Telephone: 0141–554 5669

Appendix 3

Practical help and support for families

ChildLine is a children's helpline which offers counselling and advice, particularly for children and young people who are suffering abuse. Telephone 0800 1111

Contact A Family supports parents who have children with a disability. Telephone their national office on 0171-383 3555.

EPOCH (End Physical Punishment of Children): the campaign offers advice and information plus relevant literature: telephone 0171-700 0627.

The Family Rights Group is a national organisation which works to improve law and practice with regard to families. It can be contacted on 0171-923 2628 and also runs an advice line for those offering support to families in contact with social services. This advice line is open from Monday to Friday from 1.30–3.30 pm on 0171-249 0008.

Gingerbread is an organisation offering support to lone parent families. The national organisation on 0171-240 0953 can put you in touch with your local group.

The **NSPCC** is the national voluntary organisation concerned with protecting children from abuse. The NSPCC runs a Freephone Helpline on 0800 800 500. This helpline is open 24-hours-a-day, and every day of the year. If you have a concern about a child, whether your own or someone else's, they will be happy to either advise or direct you on to other sources of help.

NAPSAC is a national organisation offering information and advice to anyone concerned about a child (or adult) with learning disabilities who may be involved in sexual abuse. They can be contacted on 0115-970 9987.

Parentline offers telephone advice and a network of local self-help groups. A national contact point can put you in touch with your nearest locally-based Parentline telephone support link – telephone 01702-559900

Local sources of help:

Appendix 4

Resources for your community

Books

Books can be useful in a variety of ways. If you wish to extend your understanding of the subject of abuse, you will find it useful to turn to Appendix 5.

Books can be a great source of support and information if they are of the right kind and accessible. There are several books which may be useful in a church library or as a resource for individuals who have experienced abuse, or as a help to those who may respond to abused children and adults.

Books with children in mind

Many books designed for children may be suitable for an open book shelf for young people. There are a large number of books published for children which deal with risk, and ways of avoiding it. *Feeling Happy, Feeling Safe* by Michele Elliot, is a colour picture book suitable for ages 3–6 years, and *The Willow Street Kids* by the same author is written for children aged 6–11 years. An up-to-date list of suitable Kidscape publications can be obtained by ringing 0171-730 3300.

The Children's Society publish some imaginative books for children of different ages. Ring 0171-837 4299 for further details.

A book which is more suitable for older children with experience of abuse, is *Out in the open* by Bain and Sanders, 1990 Virago Upstarts, a book written for young people. The authors and contributors talk frankly about the experience of sexual abuse and offer practical advice to survivors of abuse, families and helpers.

Books for adults

There are several books written by adults who have been abused and many more which are accounts of the experience of abuse by survivors. Most are about sexual abuse. Although we list them for adults, older adolescents with this experience may also find them very helpful.

Outgrowing Pain – a book for and about adults abused as children by Eliana Gil, 1983, Dell Publishing Company, New York, is a book which addresses some of the issues for those who have been victims of abuse and is suitable for older adolescents.

The Courage to Heal: For women and men survivors of childhood sexual abuse by Laura David and Ellen Bass, 1990, Cedar (Mandarin Paperbacks), has an accompanying workbook by Laura Davis which is also useful.

There are a growing number of publications which deal with those who abuse children, in particular those who sexually abuse children. Most are intended for a professional audience. Titles can be obtained from a specialist book service or major bookshop.

The important topic of the abuse of children and young adults with disabilities is receiving increasing attention. We recommend *Violence and Abuse in the Lives of People with Disabilities* by Dick Sobsey, published by Paul H Brookes in 1994. This is a powerful book which gives a vivid picture of the vulnerability of people with disabilities to abuse of all kinds. A book which reviews current research on this subject is *Abuse of Children and Adults with Disabilities* by Helen Westcott published by the NSPCC 1993.

For those who wish to follow up the research foundation for the factual information given in *Taking Care*, we suggest that the National Children's Bureau's series of *Highlights* is the best source. At only £2.00 each at the time of going to press, these publications summarise and reference research publications in an accessible form. The four *Highlights* which are most relevant are no. 119 *Child Sexual Abuse*, no. 139 *Children and Domestic Violence*, no. 143 *Children With Disabilities and Child Protection*, and nos. 148/9 *Parental Psychiatric Disorder and Child Maltreatment*, Parts I and II.

Books for parents

For parents who wish to talk to their children there is *Keeping Safe: A practical guide to talking with children* by Michele Elliott, Bedford Square Press. Kidscape (tel. 0171-730 3300) produce a helpful booklet for parents entitled *Why My Child?* which is a guide for parents whose children have been sexually abused.

NSPCC (tel. 0171-825 2500) publishes booklets for parents, particularly on how to cope with stress and how to keep babies and children safe. Churches may wish to stock these and other books and pamphlets mentioned in this section.

Videos

Using a video can be a powerful and effective way of helping people understand the experience of abuse. Before you take the responsibility of showing a video to any group, it is important to have viewed it yourself in preparation. It is always important to show videos in small supportive groups where discussion and sharing of feelings are possible. It is also important to follow up such meetings with personal support for any individual for whom the material raises difficult issues.

For adults

To A Safer Place, an award winning Canadian video (available from Educational Media International, 235 Imperial Drive, Rayners Lane, Harrow, Middlesex HA2 7HE; hire price £30 at time of press) is an account of the sexual abuse of Shirley Turcotte who goes back to her home neighbourhood and reflects on the effect of the abuse on her and her family including her brothers and sister. The video also discusses why neighbours did not intervene.

It may be useful to explore too, the attitudes and behaviour of those who abuse. A video tape included in the Kidscape pack *Protecting Children* (p. 59) gives a chilling insight into the views and behaviour of a small number of adults who systematically sexually abuse children. A short clip from this video will certainly mean that strong feelings about abuse will emerge. It may also mean that a fuller picture is drawn of the challenges faced by those who wish to protect children.

For young people

There are a number of videos made with young people in mind, usually designed to help children protect themselves against abuse.

Feeling Yes, Feeling No (available from Educational Media International see above) is a set of four Canadian videos for different age groups with detailed notes, focusing on self-protection from abuse, primarily sexual abuse.

Another video, *Good Things Still Happen*, available from International Media International, is a cartoon format for younger viewers.

Appendix 5

Going further

You may want to go further in your understanding of child abuse or the situation of children in our society.

To do so you will need to give attention to three areas, the balance between them depending upon your own interests and situation.

The three areas are:
- Exploring feelings and attitudes;
- Gaining information;
- Developing skills.

The Open University material to which we will refer below, calls these stages 'feel, think, do'.

We list here publications which will be useful to you. Some of these publications will be available through your local library; all should be obtainable on order through a good bookshop; if you cannot obtain them through these channels there are specialist bookshops (Abbey Books for example 01332-290021); some will be available for reference in specialist libraries in universities and childcare agencies.

Exploring feelings and attitudes

To gain a greater insight into what abuse can mean, it is helpful to turn to autobiographical accounts, poems or novels about abuse. There are a number of autobiographical accounts of the experience of sexual abuse in particular, including Jacqueline Spring's *Cry Hard and Swim* 1987 from Virago, and *My Father's House* by Sylvia Fraser 1989 also from Virago. *The Bone People* by Keri Hulme is an award-winning novel about physical abuse. Many readers find it an illuminating insight into the complexities of abuse situations, including the feelings and experience of both the abuser and the abused child.

The videos listed in Appendix 4 are also valuable in giving more sensitive insights into the individual experience of abuse for a child and for ensuring that learning about abuse is grounded in understanding and feelings.

Gaining information

The best way of gaining information for many people is reading about a subject area. You may be lucky in having local expertise you can draw on as well but broader background reading is always helpful.

We can recommend the course reader from the Open University training package. This course reader entitled *Child Abuse and Neglect: An introduction* is a collection of short chapters on different aspects of abuse and how we think about abuse, and provides a useful introduction to child abuse in general and the position of children in society. It will give you a grounding in understanding abuse in general and is obtainable through bookshops.

There have been important recent shifts in the way professionals respond to suspected child abuse. The major factor in creating these changes – which have been to more support for families and less focus on incidents of abuse – was the publication of *Child Protection: Messages From Research* in 1995. This book can be strongly recommended for those who wish to gain a fuller understanding of the professional response and the experience of children and families. It is published by The Stationery Office, telephone number 0171-873 9090.

Developing skills

When talking about the kinds of skills you may want to develop, it is important to be clear about what these skills are for. It is not the job of any individual in their personal capacity to investigate suspected abuse. Nor is it the role of any church member whatever their position. The task of investigation belongs to the professional agencies.

However, ongoing help needed by either child or an adult survivor of abuse may be offered by an informed lay person. Help of this kind will often be practical but may also include offering the child or adult the chance to talk about their experiences and feelings. For help in developing listening and counselling skills, books are not enough. You will need to go on a course where teaching and feedback on your progress is available. Locally there may be courses run by Relate or by Cruse, both of which are voluntary organisations which offer counselling and counselling training. Your local college or WEA may provide such courses. Courses leading to recognised qualifications are regularly advertised in the national press. It is always important to bear in mind the stress involved in hearing about abuse, sexual abuse in particular. If you do decide to learn more about counselling in this area, take care that you give yourself enough personal support.

General training packages

Some training packages have been produced which provide material in all the fields mentioned above. Notably there is the Open University package *Child abuse and neglect: an introduction.* This pack is obtainable in different forms depending upon your needs whether as an individual student or for a group. The pack as a whole is expensive but where a group of churches club together to carry out a programme of learning it may be possible to afford the whole package and work through the different kinds of activity and workbooks which it contains. It is a very substantial publication and provides material which will underpin a considerable learning programme. It is available from Learning Materials Services Office, The Open University, PO Box 188, Milton Keynes MK7 6D8. Telephone 01908-653338 (24 hours).

The Kidscape publication *Protecting Children* provides a useful general package which is less expensive and includes a wide variety of information and activities plus a video (The Stationery Office 0171-873 0011).

A training package has recently been produced dealing with the abuse of children with disabilities. This publication *Abuse and Children who are Disabled*; *the ABCD pack* is available from the NSPCC Training Centre, Beaumont Leys, Leicester. Telephone 01533-340804.

Members of faith communities who are working with children, both in day care groups and community groups, will find the National Children's Bureau publication *Managing to Change – Module 5: Child Protection* very helpful. Published in 1997, it is specifically aimed at people who work with children under eight years old, but offers a range of activities which can be easily adapted for use with people working with after school groups, holiday groups or any children's groups run in faith communities. It also considers difficult topics such as how we might deal with a situation where we suspect a colleague may be abusing a child, and how we can come to terms with the feelings left after a child protection investigation. It is available from Book Sales, National Children's Bureau, 8 Wakley Street, London EC1V 7QE. Tel: 0171-843 6028/29.

These organisations were involved in the development of the original edition of *Taking Care.*

Barnardos

The Children's Society

MAKING LIVES WORTH LIVING

A VOLUNTARY SOCIETY OF THE CHURCH OF ENGLAND AND THE CHURCH IN WALES

DEY

The Methodist Church
Division of Education and Youth

The Mothers' Union

INCORPORATED BY ROYAL CHARTER

NCEC

National Christian Education Council

NCH

Religious Society of Friends (Quakers)

THE SALVATION ARMY

Children & Parliament is now available on the Internet. The website at `candp.ncb.org.uk` is updated weekly during the parliamentary year, with the full text of each record accessible via the government's own *Hansard* website or the National Children's Bureau Library's back-up document service.

Children & Parliament is an annotated subject listing of items taken daily from the pages of the Lords and Commons *Hansard*. It includes Questions, Motions and Debates, and the passage of Bills and Regulations.

Subjects cover everything from sex offender registration to housing policy, disability rights to specific learning difficulties, social security benefit entitlement to social exclusion, or family breakdown to the decriminalisation of drugs.

Children & Parliament ensures that you are comprehensively briefed on all the issues affecting children and young people. We review the latest government consultation documents as well as the pre-publication pronouncements, follow legislation as it wends its way through both Houses and Committees, examine the politicians' arguments in favour of their most recent causes – and try to make some sense of it all!

Annual subscription to Children & Parliament (ISSN 1406-9010)
£40 Bureau members, £65 Non-members *

To subscribe, contact the Library & Information Service on e-mail: library@ncb.org.uk. Tel: 0171 843 6035/6037, Fax: 0171 843 6007, or write to the Library & Information Service, National Children's Bureau, 8 Wakley Street, London EC1V 7QE.

* If you would like to know more about the benefits of becoming a Member of the Bureau, please contact Jane Lewis, Membership Marketing Coordinator, on 0171 843 6047.

The full index to Children & Parliament from Oct 1990 is available on ChildData, the Bureau's CD-ROM. Details are available from Oxmill Publishing (www.headfast.co.uk; Tel: +44(0)1883 343000; Fax: +44(0)1883 349777; e-mail: sales@headfast.co.uk)

Children & Parliament

NATIONAL CHILDREN'S BUREAU

The powerful voice for the child